TERRORISM

BLAIRSVILLE SENIOR HIGH SCHOOL
BLAIRSVILLE, PENNA.

© Aladdin Books Ltd

All rights reserved

Designed and produced by
Aladdin Books Ltd
70 Old Compton Street
London W1

*First published in the
United States in 1986 by*
Gloucester Press
387 Park Avenue South
New York NY 10016

ISBN 0-531-17030-6

Printed in Belgium

Library of Congress Catalog
Card Number: 86-80629

The front cover photograph shows a terrorist incident
in the streets of Beirut, Lebanon. The back cover
photograph shows a political mural in Belfast,
Northern Ireland.

*The author, Dr Christopher Coker, is a lecturer in International
Relations at the London School of Economics, London, UK.*

*The consultant, Dr John Pimlott, is Senior Lecturer in the
Department of War Studies and International Affairs, RMA,
Sandhurst, UK.*

Contents

TERRORISM

CHRISTOPHER COKER

Illustrated by
Ron Hayward Associates

Gloucester Press
New York : Toronto : 1986

Introduction

Every month we read of outrages committed all over the world: 150 vacationers taken hostage on a cruise liner in the Mediterranean; an airplane hijacked in Beirut; an attempt to blow up the entire British government when a bomb explodes. These events are examples of political violence: they are acts of terrorism.

By selecting specific targets, such as aircraft, stores or terminals, terrorists want to show that the state cannot protect its citizens. By doing this, they hope to create a climate of fear which makes normal living conditions impossible.

▽ Beirut airport, Lebanon, June 1985: a hijacked Jordanian aircraft burns after being blown up by Muslim terrorists. Disturbing evidence of the growth of terrorism, such sights have become quite frequent in certain parts of the world.

Terrorist organizations use terror *itself* as a device to create fear and panic, not just in a government or a social group but in the whole population. Terrorists' actions are criminal and may seem random, but they are not mindless.

World governments do not yet know how to deal with the problem: one man's terrorist is another man's freedom fighter. As long as the world is unable to agree on a common definition of terrorism, it is unlikely to act decisively against it. As a result, terrorism is growing and has become one of today's most frightening problems.

Escalation

Terrorism is not new – the first historically recognized terrorist incidents occurred in the 19th century – but it has grown dramatically in the last 20 years. Since the 1970s, the world has seen an alarming increase in the number of terrorist movements and in the actual methods they use.

This growth is partly because terrorists help each other. But another factor has become significant: publicity on an international scale. Television coverage has enabled terrorist ideas to travel from country to country, producing new organizations. For example, in the United States, the Black Panthers produced the White Panthers, and the Tupamaros in Uruguay inspired the creation of the Tupamaros in West Berlin.

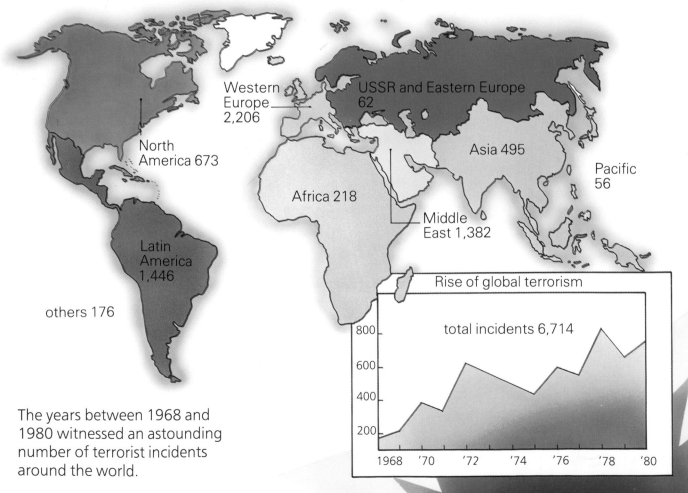

Western Europe 2,206

USSR and Eastern Europe 62

North America 673

Asia 495

Africa 218

Pacific 56

Middle East 1,382

Latin America 1,446

others 176

Rise of global terrorism

total incidents 6,714

800
600
400
200

1968   '70   '72   '74   '76   '78   '80

The years between 1968 and 1980 witnessed an astounding number of terrorist incidents around the world.

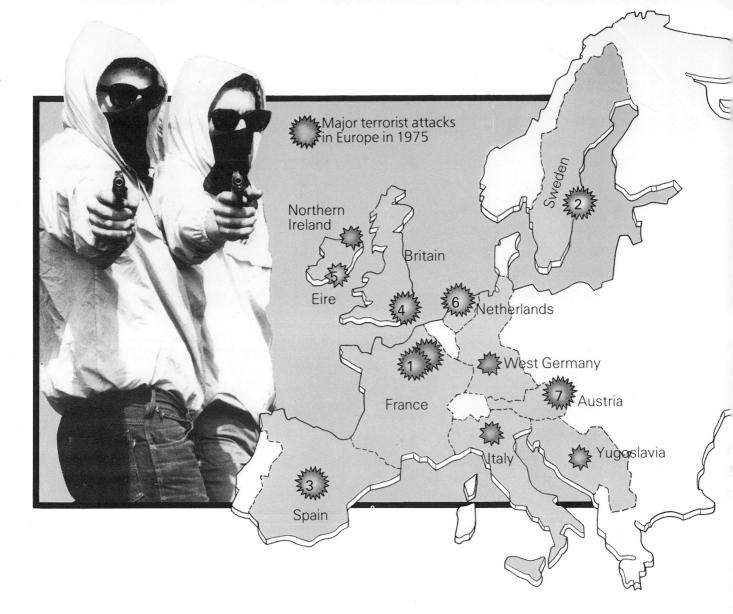

Major terrorist attacks in Europe in 1975

International publicity has also led terrorist groups to copy each other's methods, so that along with such traditional terrorist practices as assassination and hostage taking, the world is now witnessing more hijacking of aircraft and embassy sieges. The hijacking of American aircraft to Cuba, for example, was imitated around the world, reaching a peak of 82 such incidents in 1969. The kidnapping of the US ambassador in Brazil, in September 1969, was copied by so many groups that between 1969-75 there was an attempted kidnapping of an American diplomat once every three months, and a successful kidnapping once every five!

Both in its scale and scope, the world had never seen anything like this kind of terrorist activity before. However, we must not exaggerate its impact: it did not bring society to a halt.

△ 1975 was a fairly typical year for terrorist attacks. Among the many incidents in Europe, some of the major examples were: (1) two attempts to shoot down airliners leaving Orly airport (Paris, France); the seizure of embassies in (2) Stockholm (Sweden) and (3) Madrid (Spain); (4) an IRA bombing campaign in London (UK) and (5) the kidnapping of a Dutch businessman in Eire; (6) the hijacking of a train by South Moluccan terrorists in the Netherlands and (7) the kidnapping of Arab oil ministers at a meeting in Vienna (Austria).

Why terrorism?

People who turn to political violence do so for various reasons. In many countries, it is because they find themselves in conflict with what they think are unjust, repressive governments, or perhaps because they come from underprivileged social groups.

However, in Western societies this is not the case. A recent study found that 90 per cent of the members of European terrorist movements are intelligent young people from middle-class families. They become terrorists as a means of *political* expression. They are opposed to capitalist society – one which places great importance on material values. However, there are other reasons to explain why people turn to terrorism.

The Baader-Meinhof gang
The Baader-Meinhof gang in West Germany, known as the Red Army Faction (RAF), is the classic example of a group of disenchanted young people who turned to terrorism in the early 1970s. Ulrike Meinhof, Andreas Baader and Gudrun Ensslin were founder members of the gang. Trained by the PLO in Lebanon, the gang carried out a number of embassy sieges and spectacular kidnappings. Hanns-Martin Schleyer (photograph left) was one such victim, kidnapped in 1977 and subsequently murdered. Most of the leaders committed suicide in prison. They were aided by their lawyers who smuggled in the arms.

Elsewhere in the world, people who are part of discontented ethnic groups within a country turn to terrorism for reasons of *nationalism*. They want to establish their own nation and win freedom and independence.

More recently, we have seen the gradual emergence of a new form of terrorism which is *religious*, rather than political or nationalist in inspiration. Throughout the Middle East, Muslim groups have begun to fight for the creation of a society which is less Westernized and closer to their religion. Like the other forms of terrorism, however, it represents the need of many people to find some spiritual purpose in an extremely materialistic age.

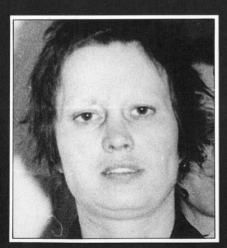  

Ulrike Meinhof (1934-76) was the daughter of an art historian and a graduate in philosophy and sociology. In the 1960s, she was a writer for left-wing magazines. She rescued Andreas Baader from prison in 1970. Captured by the police, she committed suicide in 1976.

Andreas Baader (1943-77) was the son of a historian. He was sentenced to three years imprisonment for a bomb attack in Frankfurt at the height of the student unrest in the late 1960s. Rescued in 1970, he established contact with the PLO. He committed suicide with Ensslin in 1977.

Gudrun Ensslin (1940-77) was a clergyman's daughter and a graduate in philosophy and languages. She was sentenced with Baader for the Frankfurt attack. She received training from the PLO. After receiving a life sentence in 1977 for several crimes, she too committed suicide.

Democracy under threat

Democratic countries — where governments genuinely represent the people who elect them — are especially vulnerable to terrorist attacks. One reason for this is that these countries are mostly in the western, industrialized world, where the complexity of modern society provides many vulnerable targets. Reservoirs can be poisoned, electricity systems can be put out of action, or trains carrying nuclear waste can be derailed.

Democracies are more vulnerable still because the media is not censored. Terrorism *needs* publicity to make its impact, and television, in particular, provides it. Television reports events and is also used to show actual terrorist incidents.

▽ On December 19, 1985, Arab and French terrorists held a court at gunpoint in Nantes, France for over two days. The whole episode was captured on television. Indeed, the terrorists actually *used* the cameras to get their message across to the nation.

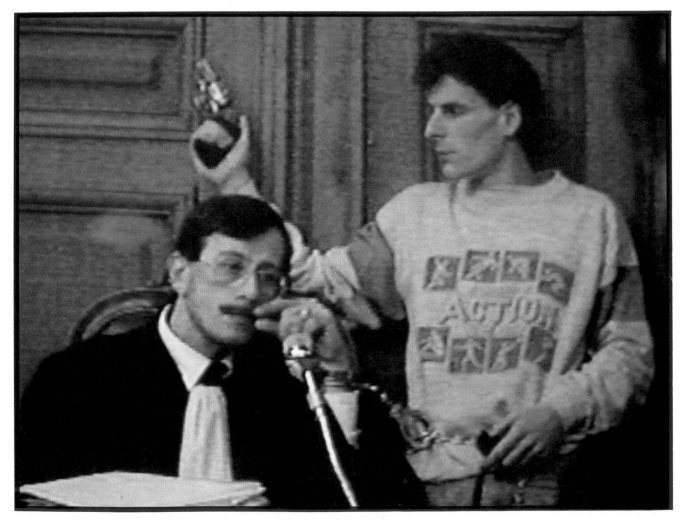

The murder of the Israeli athletes at the 1972 Munich Olympic Games was watched by a horrified audience of 500 million people. Television has also been used by terrorists to put over their cases in interviews, and even to show video-taped recordings of victims confessing to alleged "crimes against the people."

Democratic governments are also exposed to terrorism because they tend to be more sensitive toward public opinion. Consequently, to ensure that they are not being pushed into extreme measures which would threaten the rights and freedom of their own citizens, they are more likely to show restraint in combating terrorism.

▽ The introduction in the mid-1970s of the portable video recorder and lightweight camera have made it much easier to make "instant news" of terrorist actions. This dramatic example is taken from a television interview with a hijacker at Beirut airport in 1985. The TWA pilot, John Testrake, displayed remarkable courage throughout his ordeal.

Capitalist societies

△ The destruction of public buildings is one of the most indiscriminate forms of terrorist action. A dramatic example was the bombing of the Bologna, Italy, train station in 1980. This outrage is generally believed to have been carried out by *right-wing* terrorists. Although fewer in number than *left-wing* organizations, right-wing terrorist groups are nevertheless as ruthless in their use of violence.

Modern capitalist societies in North America and Western Europe have produced by far the most extreme terrorist movements. These organizations aim at the destruction of capitalist society. In the United States, for example, a terrorist group called the Weathermen set out to destroy the capitalist system, attacking banks and companies. In 15 months they used no less than 4,300 incendiary bombs.

The members of such organizations usually come from prosperous, middle-class homes.

Nevertheless, they identify with the "exploited" working class. Some groups, like the Red Brigade in Italy, hold politicians and bankers in "people's prisons," where they are tried and often "executed" for crimes against the working class.

However, these groups have found little support. Their actions have been condemned by socialist parties and trade unions. Such terrorist groups are protesting against a lifestyle and living standards which the working classes worked hard to have a share in.

△ Two members of the Red Brigade are photographed above in prison. This organization has tried to end capitalism in Italy. It has been responsible for attacks on factories and communications and the kidnapping and murder of former Prime Minister Aldo Moro. Moro was forced to admit to "crimes against the people," in a video message to the nation.

Ireland and the IRA

	troop levels
	terrorist incidents

21,200
12,481
13,452
9,090
1,503
592
1972
1978
1984

△ In terms of terrorist incidents and troop levels, the situation in Northern Ireland has improved since 1972.

The Irish Republican Army (IRA) has been campaigning to unify Ireland since 1922. Far from seeing itself as a terrorist organization, it claims it is fighting a war against an occupying force – the British. It hopes the British government will eventually respond to the sheer cost of maintaining order in Northern Ireland – both in terms of lives and money – by pulling out.

So in order to increase the running costs of Northern Ireland's union with Britain, the IRA began a successful campaign in 1969 to bring down the regional government of Northern Ireland and to force the British government to impose direct rule. As part of its aim to increase the cost in human lives, it has continued to attack the British army that was sent in 1969 as a peacekeeping force.

△ The IRA bombing of a hotel in Brighton, England, in 1984 was an attempt to assassinate the entire British government, who were attending a conference there. They failed to kill a single senior cabinet member, but four people died and a further 32 were injured.

◁ The IRA views itself as a paramilitary force, the military arm of the Sinn Fein, not a classic terrorist movement. Consequently, IRA members wear military uniforms on parade and fire volleys of ammunition at IRA funerals.

When it became obvious that the British were not going to pull out, the IRA turned its attention to the British people on the mainland, with a random bombing campaign. The IRA also resorted to political assassination, from the murder of a cousin of the Queen, in 1979, to the attempted assassination of all the key members of the British government in 1984. Alongside these acts of political violence, the movement is now also using its political wing, Sinn Fein, to compete in local and national elections.

The IRA has not succeeded in achieving its main objectives. However, it has succeeded in further dividing the Protestant and Catholic communities. This has made it increasingly difficult for the British government to introduce certain political reforms which might restore the faith of the Catholics in the union with Britain.

16

Palestinian terrorism

◁ In acts of indiscriminate violence, terrorists machine-gunned innocent passengers waiting at El Al check-in desks at airports in Rome and Vienna in December 1985.

▽ With the declaration of the state of Israel in 1948, thousands of Palestinians left the country and settled in refugee camps throughout the Middle East. Today their numbers have increased significantly. Inevitably, this has led to friction with local populations. In 1970, the Palestinians were forced out of Jordan and in 1982 they were expelled from Lebanon by an invading Israeli force.

The Palestine Liberation Organization (PLO) was founded in 1964 to campaign for a homeland for the Palestinian people. Convinced it could not rely on its Arab neighbors for help, it turned to political violence to achieve its aims.

The PLO, however, has never claimed to be a terrorist movement, but a national liberation movement. In this it has been so successful that in 1974 its chairman, Yasser Arafat, was invited to address the UN General Assembly.

Unfortunately, as the organization has won international respectability, it has also unwittingly provoked many of its more extreme members to leave and set up independent terrorist organizations. The Popular Democratic Front for the Liberation of Palestine (PDFLP) and the Black September group are two major examples, and a more recent example is Abu Nidal's organization, responsible for the Rome and Vienna massacres.

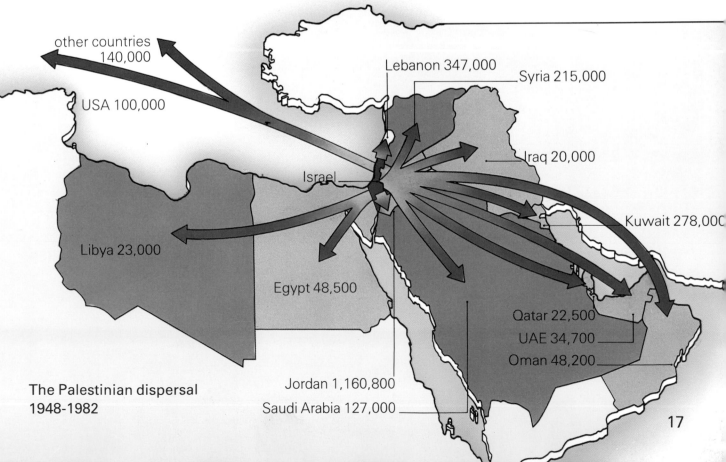

other countries 140,000

USA 100,000

Lebanon 347,000

Syria 215,000

Iraq 20,000

Israel

Kuwait 278,000

Libya 23,000

Egypt 48,500

Qatar 22,500

UAE 34,700

Oman 48,200

The Palestinian dispersal 1948-1982

Jordan 1,160,800

Saudi Arabia 127,000

Islamic terrorism

Particularly bewildering to Western observers is a new phenomenon — religious terrorism. Its inspiration was the revolution in Iran in 1978-79, which brought to power a new government, headed by militant religious leaders, or "mullahs." Inspired by the Islamic faith and the promise that martyrs will win a privileged place in heaven, these terrorists have been among the most fanatical of all.

They have built up a complex international network and have begun to forge links with European terrorist organizations such as the Red Brigade.

△ Islamic terrorists include children 15 years old. These children, inspired by religious zeal, have blown themselves up in attacks. Their video-taped messages to the nation were played on Lebanese television after their deaths.

The main battleground for these beliefs is Lebanon, once the most prosperous and tolerant state in the Middle East, which collapsed into civil war in the mid-1970s. Here terrorists have engaged in a particularly devastating form of violence – car bombings aimed at innocent civilians and embassy compounds.

The most militant group of all, the Islamic Holy War, considers the United States to be the main source of Western influence in the Middle East, and therefore the main threat to Islam. Consequently, in their attacks, US citizens are deliberately singled out.

▽ The two most devastating car bomb attacks were carried out in 1983, against the command posts of the US and French peacekeeping forces in Lebanon. 241 US servicemen and 58 French soldiers were killed.

Latin America

The conditions which breed political violence in Latin America are unique. It is one of the poorest regions in the world, where cities have grown faster than anywhere else, creating vast slums.

So it is not surprising that the terrorists' targets have been the symbols of wealth in a land of poverty: landowners, businessmen and foreign companies, mostly American – are all alleged to exploit the peasants. Through their actions, these terrorist groups hope to make the people aware of their wretched conditions and be prepared to act to change it.

▽ In Latin America, terrorists are dealing with often harsh military governments. These regimes are often prepared to resort to terrorism themselves. In Argentina, the police formed "murder squads," which eliminated over 20,000 suspected terrorist supporters. In Uruguay, the Tupamaros were virtually wiped out, by which time, however, one in ten Uruguayan citizens was in jail.

Here, kidnapping is one of the most commonly used tactics, both for political reasons and because it helps to bring in funds. Such funds enabled one terrorist group, the Tupamaros in Uruguay, to achieve enough publicity and popularity to be able to blackmail companies into distributing free food and free medical supplies to hospitals.

The kidnapping of businessmen began in 1971, and the present ransom record is a staggering $60 million, paid to the Argentinian group, the "Montoneros," for two hostages in 1974.

▽ The sight of terrorists who have died at the army's hands is a frequent one in many Latin American countries. Often the dead are left where they have been killed, to discourage others from joining terrorist movements. The cans on the back of the truck are actually home-made bombs.

Global links

All terrorists believe in world revolution and so their organizations help each other throughout the world and involve themselves in each other's causes. They provide other groups with forged passports and visas so that they can travel more easily and even with arms and training. The PLO, for example, has trained Basque terrorists in Yemen, the Baader-Meinhof gang in Lebanon, and also the Black Panthers. It has even trained right-wing, neo-Nazi German groups. Terrorists have also cooperated in actual operations, such as the attack on Lod airport in Tel Aviv, Israel, in 1972.

This international network is now extensive and is still growing. However, it makes the groups vulnerable. The links can be broken in any part of the chain – the more information they share, the harder it is to keep secret – and the movements can also be penetrated more easily by the police.

victims from Puerto Rico

masterminded by Carlos from Venezuela

◁ "Carlos" is the name used by a Venezuelan terrorist with extensive international contacts. He was trained in Cuba in terrorist tactics in the 1960s, sponsored by the KGB, the Soviet Secret Service. In 1970 he made contact with the leaders of the Baader-Meinhof gang. In 1975 he took over a PLO group operating in Paris. The seizure of Arab oil ministers in Vienna two years later was masterminded by Carlos, aided by the Baader-Meinhof gang. After the Vienna raid, Carlos disappeared from the active terrorist scene in Europe, hunted by the world's police.

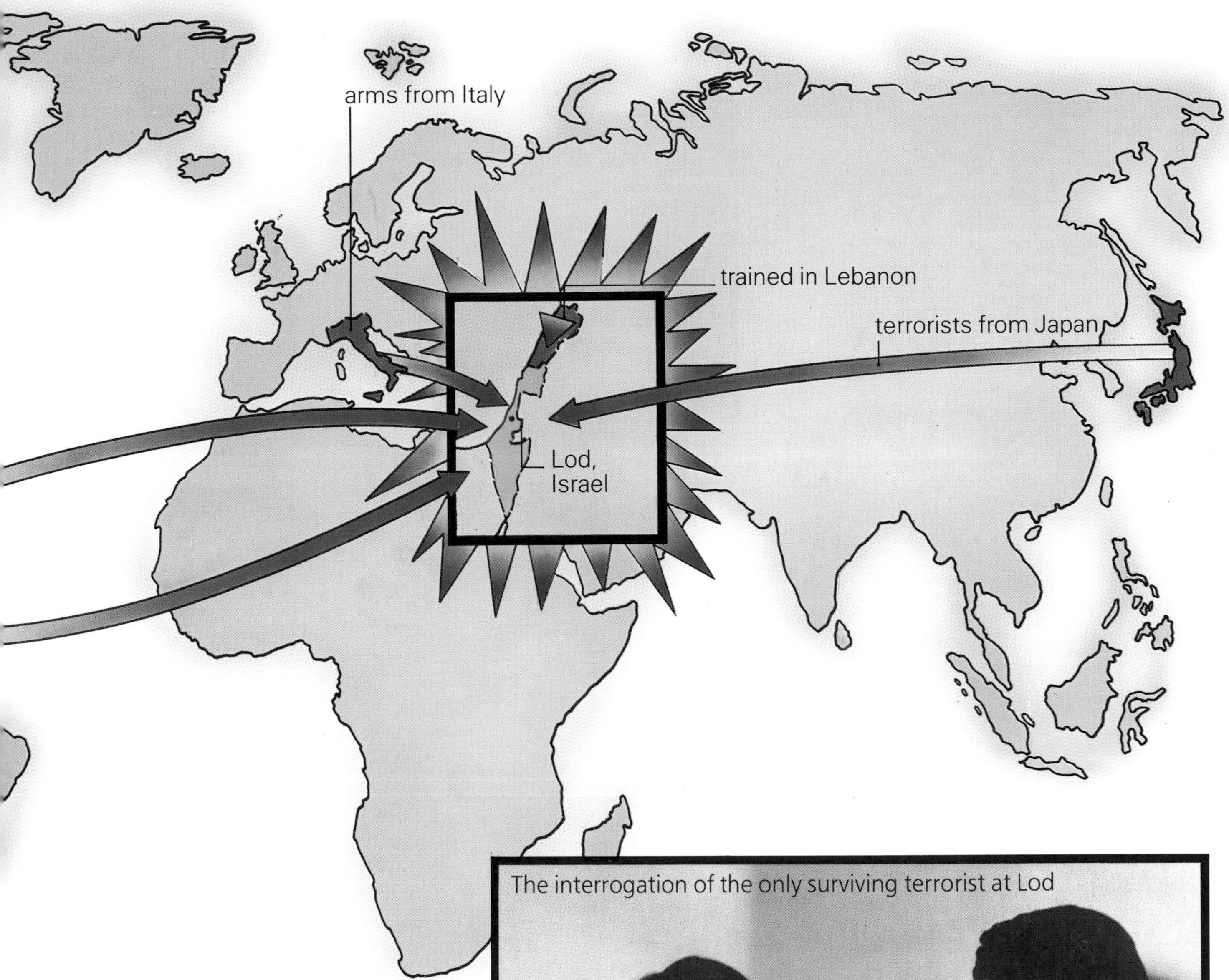

arms from Italy

trained in Lebanon

terrorists from Japan

Lod,
Israel

The interrogation of the only surviving terrorist at Lod

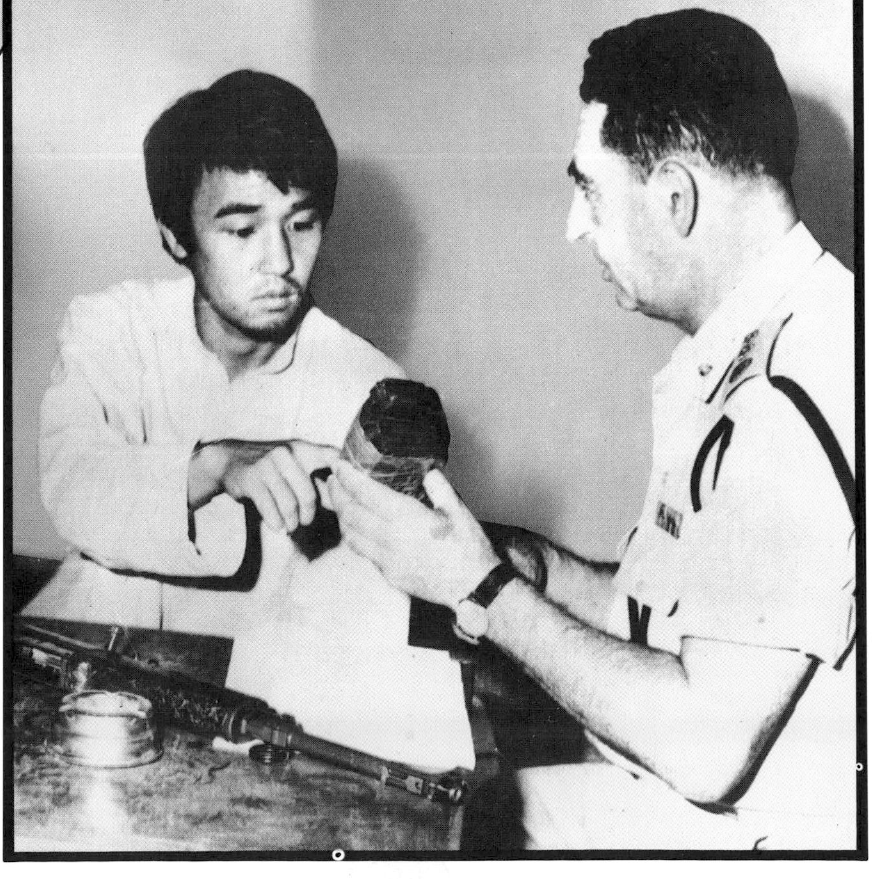

△ In 1972, the Japanese Red
Army attacked Lod airport in
Israel to win publicity for its
cause. 27 people died in the
attack, most of them Puerto
Ricans on a pilgrimage to
Jerusalem. The terrorists were
trained by the PLO in Lebanon
and were armed with weapons
that had been delivered to
Rome. The whole operation
was masterminded by the
Venezuelan terrorist leader,
"Carlos."

Anti-terrorist action

The bungled attempt of the West German police to rescue the Israeli athletes at the Munich Olympics in 1972 ended in the deaths of all 11 athletes concerned. This fiasco, and the steady growth of terrorism in the 1970s, illustrated the need for world governments to set up special groups to combat terrorism.

Some groups, like the GSG-9 in West Germany, are specialist police units. Others, like the SAS (Special Air Services) in Britain, are made up of regular army personnel. Squads drawn from the Italian Carabinieri are independent paramilitary forces. In such groups, members are carefully selected and specially trained.

△ The badge above sums up the total commitment of the SAS in fighting world terrorism.

▽ Members of anti-terrorist squads take part in rigorous training exercises.

▽ Governments have been forced to act decisively in forming anti-terrorist squads partly because of embassy sieges. Of the 550 terrorist incidents between 1979-81, diplomats and diplomatic property were involved in over 200. The success record in dealing with such incidents has been mixed. However, in the Iranian embassy siege in London, 1980 (photographed below) the SAS succeeded in rescuing diplomats held by Arab terrorists, without the loss of a single hostage.

Training is both physical and psychological. It includes unarmed combat, the use of special weapons like stun grenades (an SAS speciality) and a knowledge of explosives and marksmanship. In addition, all special forces are trained in basic bargaining skills, in the hope of talking terrorists out of difficult situations.

Certain countries have gone further in their anti-terrorist action. For example, in April 1986 the United States bombed Tripoli and Benghazi in Libya. This was in response to Libyan-backed terrorist attacks on American tourists and soldiers in Europe earlier in the year. Such actions meet with mixed reaction around the world.

A success story

In 1977, a Lufthansa aircraft was hijacked by Palestinians in support of the Baader-Meinhof gang. The West German anti-terrorist squad, the GSG-9, went into action, aided by two British SAS men. Some 40 minutes before the deadline for the release of the Meinhof gang, 28 German commandos forced the main door of the aircraft in Mogadishu, Somalia. They killed three of the hijackers outright and rescued the hostages. The whole operation lasted only 11 minutes.

An alternative to force in such situations is negotiation. Many countries try to prolong hostage situations, in the hope of persuading terrorists to give up. At one time it was not unknown for a personal bond to be established between hostages and their captors.

Today, however, to prevent such situations from arising, terrorists have begun to work in small groups, dehumanizing their victims by forcing them to remain silent, often blindfolding them, and wearing hoods themselves. As the Mogadishu incident showed when the terrorist leader "executed" the German pilot, terrorists are prepared to kill hostages to break a deadlock in negotiations, or to prove their seriousness.

The Mogadishu rescue

Before the successful outcome of the Mogadishu rescue, many complex maneuvers took place over several days. On October 13, 1977, the aircraft was hijacked at Palma. After refueling in Rome and Cyprus, it flew on to the Middle East. At Aden the pilot was shot. It then flew on to Mogadishu, where it landed on October 17.

Meanwhile, the first of two groups of GSG-9 men left for Cyprus, but arrived just as the hijacked aircraft took off. They returned to base via Ankara to change aircraft on October 15, then flew to Crete, and then to Mogadishu. They arrived after dark on October 17, and at 0150 hours the rescue operation began. The second group of GSG-9, including West Germany's leading trouble shooter, Hans-Jurgen Wischnewski, arrived at Dubai at dawn on October 15. Their Boeing 707 was refused permission to land in Aden and was diverted to Jiddah in Saudi Arabia. It arrived in Mogadishu on October 17 to coordinate the rescue operation.

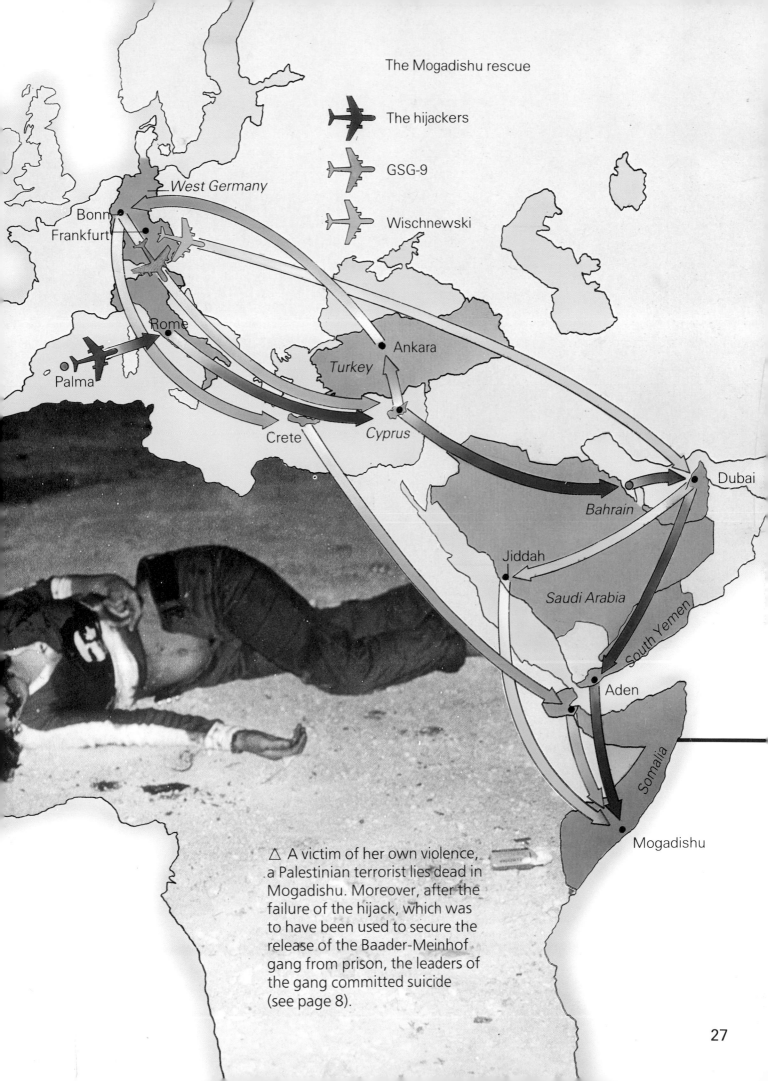

The Mogadishu rescue

The hijackers

GSG-9

Wischnewski

West Germany

Bonn
Frankfurt

Palma

Rome

Crete

Turkey

Ankara

Cyprus

Bahrain

Jiddah

Saudi Arabia

South Yemen

Aden

Somalia

Dubai

Mogadishu

△ A victim of her own violence, a Palestinian terrorist lies dead in Mogadishu. Moreover, after the failure of the hijack, which was to have been used to secure the release of the Baader-Meinhof gang from prison, the leaders of the gang committed suicide (see page 8).

Hope for the future?

▽ With the increase in aircraft hijacking in the 1970s, airport security was tightened up considerably. Armed security guards, and even armored cars outside European airport terminals, like those in the photograph below, have become common sights. The use of these and other security measures will make it increasingly difficult to smuggle weapons aboard aircraft, or to machine gun innocent passengers at check-in desks.

As a product of modern society, terrorism is here to stay. Deterrence is expensive. Therefore, success in fighting terrorism will have to depend on government countermeasures, such as intelligence gathering and monitoring dangerous situations to anticipate terrorist attacks.

Another countermeasure is to penalize countries which actively support terrorism. In a summit conference held in Japan in May 1986 the seven leading industrial nations agreed to take a tougher line against countries that back terrorist groups: Libya in particular was singled out. It is hoped that such measures will help to reduce the number of terrorist attacks in the future.

▷ To deter terrorist attacks, airports today X-ray baggage for hidden weapons.

▽ Body searches of passengers are also frequently made. However, these measures are expensive. One study found the cost of such screening in the United States, in three years alone, came to nearly $200 million.

Terrorists world-wide

Argentina

The Montoneros continue to remain Latin America's principal terrorist group, which makes its living by kidnapping Western businessmen. It first came to prominence in 1970, by kidnapping the former President Pedro Arambaru and subjecting him to a "people's trial." Although it lost many of its members in the government's anti-terrorist campaign of the late 1970s, in which over 20,000 people perished (many of whom were innocent), it is still active.

Egypt

The Muslim Brotherhood was responsible for the assassination of President Sadat in 1981. Founded in 1928, it is a radical Islamic organization that wishes to rid Egypt of Western influence. Occasionally it has contested elections as a political party, but for most of its history, it has been banned and forced underground.

France

Action Directe is an anarchist movement, founded in 1979, to bring down the French state. Inspired by the Red Brigade and the Red Army Faction, it has confined its attacks largely to symbols of state authority, such as magistrates' courts and police stations. Its most recent attacks have been on NATO depots and installations.

India

Dal Khalsa, a militant Sikh organization founded in 1979 to campaign for an independent Sikh homeland. It has planted a number of bombs on Air India flights, and is suspected of killing 329 passengers on a flight from Canada in 1985. It was also responsible for the assassination of Prime Minister Indira Gandhi in 1984.

Pakistan

The Al-Zulfikar Movement emerged in 1981 to overthrow President Zia ul-Haq. It is named after the former Prime Minister Zulfikar Ali Bhutto, who was executed in 1979 after a military coup. The group has carried out several bomb attacks, including one on Karachi National Station, as well as a number of aircraft hijacks on flights from the Middle East. It is based in Afghanistan, where it is financed by the Soviet Union.

South Africa

The African National Congress (ANC) in 1984 carried out over 40 attacks on civilian targets and on major economic targets, such as a nuclear power plant near Cape Town. Founded in 1912, it turned to violence in 1960 after all political activity by the black inhabitants of the country was prohibited. It uses terror as one tactic among many to achieve political power.

Spain

The Freedom for the Basque Homeland Movement (ETA) is, after the IRA, the most dangerous of all Western Europe's terrorist movements. In one year, 1968, it killed 350 people. Its tactics include kidnapping state officials and putting them on "trial." It conducted 60 such trials in 1978. It has also murdered high-ranking officials, especially judges. Its principal victim to date was the Spanish Prime Minister Carrero Blanco in 1973.

Sri Lanka

The Sri Lankan People's Liberation Front was founded in 1965 in support of a separate Tamil homeland. It first turned to armed struggle in 1971, carrying out attacks on 90 police stations. Recently the Tamils have followed the example of the Sikhs in sabotaging civilian airlines. A particular example was the destruction of a Boeing 747 in Sri Lanka in May 1986 in which 20 people were killed.

Thailand

The Pattani United Liberation Organization (PULO) is the most active of the country's radical Muslim groups, with over 300 members. Financed by Libya, it is not a guerrilla force, but a classical terrorist movement. It has carried out arson attacks which in 1981 claimed the lives of 50 victims, in the capital Bangkok.

Chronology

1877 The *Huascar* is hijacked, making it the first ship to be seized by a terrorist group, who were from Peru.

1881 Tsar Alexander II is assassinated in Russia by a group of terrorists.

1914 The Austro-Hungarian Archduke Franz Ferdinand is assassinated by Gavrilo Princip, a member of the Black Hand terrorist organization. This event sparks off World War I.

1937 The Geneva Convention is the first international convention on terrorism. It was triggered by the murder of King Alexander I of Yugoslavia, and the French Foreign Minister, three years before.

1954 The second convention on terrorism is held, and the proposals made have yet to be agreed to by the United Nations.

1961 The first plane hijacking to Cuba takes place.

1963 The Tokyo Air Convention is held to discuss air hijacking.

1968 The US ambassador in Guatemala is assassinated, which leads to a spate of attacks throughout the world, which claim the lives of five US ambassadors by 1980.

1970-71 First the Hague Convention and then the Montreal Convention against terrorism are held.

1972 The Israeli athletes are massacred by Arab terrorists at the Munich Olympics.

1974 The first embassy siege in The Hague takes place, carried out by the Japanese Red Army.

1978-79 A revolution in Iran topples the Shah, and brings to power a radical Islamic government. This government is committed to the use of terrorism to bring about Islamic revolution.

1983 The first major car bombing in Beirut takes place. Over 300 French and US servicemen die.

1985 The *Achille Lauro* is hijacked, the first major ship hijacking since 1961.

Turkey

The Gray Wolves were allegedly involved in the attempted assassination of Pope John Paul II in 1982. Unlike most terrorist movements, it is a right-wing organization which was founded in 1976 to engage in commando-style operations against left-wing "enemies of the state."

Yugoslavia

The Croatian Revolutionary Brotherhood has been fighting for an independent Croatian republic since 1945. It is one of the few terrorist movements to operate in a communist country. Based in Australia, it has international offices in West Germany and several other Western European countries. Its principal activity has been the murder of Yugoslav diplomats, notably the ambassador to Sweden.

31

Index

Photographic Credits:
Cover and pages 13, 14, 16, 18, 20, 21 and back cover; Frank Spooner: pages 4/5, 11 and 24; Associated Press: pages 7, 8 and 27; Stern: pages 9, 22 and 23; Photosource/Keystone: pages 10, 12, 19 and 25; John Hillelson: page 28; Zefa: page 29 (top); IAL: page 29 (bottom); Colorific.

With many thanks to:
Control Risks Information Service Ltd

PRINTED IN BELGIUM BY
proost
INTERNATIONAL BOOK PRODUCTION